JUL 2019

Fact Finders®

FULL STEAM
SOCCER

Science, Technology, Engineering, Arts,
and Mathematics of the Game

by Sean McCollum

CAPSTONE PRESS
a capstone imprint

Fact Finders Books are published by Capstone Press
1710 Roe Crest Drive, North Mankato, Minnesota 56003

www.mycapstone.com

Library of Congress Cataloging-in-Publication Data
Names: McCollum, Sean, author.
Title: Full STEAM soccer : science, technology, engineering, arts, and mathematics of the game / by Sean McCollum.
Description: North Mankato, Minnesota : Capstone Press, 2019. | Series: Fact finders. Full STEAM sports | Audience: Age 8–14.
Identifiers: LCCN 2018016133 (print) | LCCN 2018019632 (ebook) | ISBN 9781543530483 (eBook PDF) | ISBN 9781543530407 (hardcover) | ISBN 9781543530445 (pbk.)
Subjects: LCSH: Soccer—Juvenile literature. | Sports sciences—Juvenile literature. | Sports—Technological innovations—Juvenile literature. Classification: LCC GV943.25 (ebook) | LCC GV943.25 .M32 2019 (print) | DDC 796.334—dc23
LC record available at https://lccn.loc.gov/2018016133

Editorial Credits
Editor: Nate LeBoutillier
Designer: Terri Poburka
Media Researcher: Eric Gohl
Production Specialist: Kris Wilfahrt

Photo Credits
Alamy: Gualtiero Boffi, 20, Kumar Sriskandan, 4; AP Photo: Anne M. Peterson, 15; Dreamstime: Alexandre Durão, 21 (top), Cosmin Iftode, 25; Getty Images: Al Tielemans, 10, 11, Bob Rosato, 28, Shaun Botterill, 9, Simon Bruty, 29, Stringer/ Simon Hofmann, 18, 19, ullstein bild, 7, VI-Images, 12; iStockphoto: duncan1890, 6; Newscom: Cal Sport Media/Dom Gagne, 23, Cal Sport Media/Sportimage, 24, Icon Sportswire/Bob Kupbens, 27, Reuters/Alessandro Bianchi, 17, SIPA/Pedro Fiuza, cover, Xinhua News Agency/Liu Dawei, 22; Shutterstock: Liubov Fediashova, 21 (bottom left), urbanbuzz, 21 (bottom right)

Design Elements
Shutterstock

Printed and bound in the United States.
PA017

CONTENTS

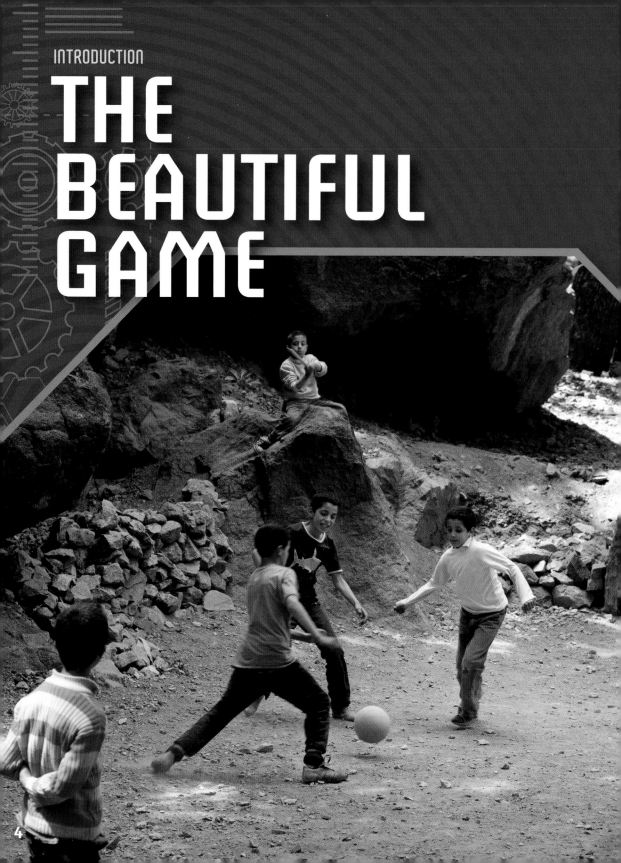

THE BEAUTIFUL GAME

More than 250 million people play soccer around the world. And every four years, the excitement for soccer unites people unlike any other sport. The World Cup brings together the best players and national teams. Fans tune in on radio, TV, and the Internet.

Soccer, or football as it is called in many places, is popular worldwide. Experts of the sport analyze it from every angle. Even science, technology, engineering, the arts, and mathematics (STEAM) have jumped into the game. These categories are more than fields of study or classes in school. They are tools for looking at the world. They also help unlock the secrets of soccer—often called "The Beautiful Game."

Soccer and Newton's Second Law of Motion

saac Newton (1643–1727) was no star soccer player. However, he is considered one of the all-time great thinkers. Newton came up with three laws of motion. They are **fundamentals** of physics—the science of energy and how various objects move, including soccer balls.

Isaac Newton

Newton's Second Law of Motion is in constant play during a soccer match. This law states, "Force equals mass times acceleration." Another way to say this is the weight (mass) of an object and its speed (acceleration) affect the amount of force the object has.

fundamental—one of the basic, important parts of something

Think of a ball blasted by Brazilian midfielder Ronny at a speed of 100 miles (161 kilometers) per hour. Now consider that same ball traveling half as fast. Which one would sting a goalie's hands more? The one that's traveling faster and is kicked with more force, right?

Ronny has blasted some of the fastest shots ever seen, some flying more than 130 miles (209 km) per hour.

A player blasts a free kick in a game. The shot looks likes it will miss the goal to the right. Suddenly, it curves back to the left and into the net. The goalkeeper is so fooled he barely moves.

What happened? Physics. Soccer players use air resistance, or **drag**, to affect how a ball moves. And by adding spin, players can cause the ball to curve in different ways.

The player had given his kick a sideways spin. At that point the **Magnus effect** went to work. Air travels differently across different sides of a spinning ball. One side moves faster with the air resistance, the other side moves slower against air resistance. The result is slightly different drag on different parts of the ball. It causes the ball to curve, or "bend" as soccer players say. The more drag and more spin, the bigger the bend.

drag—the force created when air strikes a moving object and slows it

Magnus effect— a force produced by differences in air pressure around a spinning object

Roberto Carlos bends soccer shots like a magician, using the Magnus effect.

A corner kick is an exciting play. From the corner, a player lofts the inbound pass in front of the goal. Offensive players use their heads to try to punch the ball past the goalkeeper. Defenders do the same to try to knock the ball away.

Headers require great timing and strength. However, **neurologists** say headers can cause **concussions**. Concussions are brain injuries. Most are caused by hits to, or violent shaking of, the head.

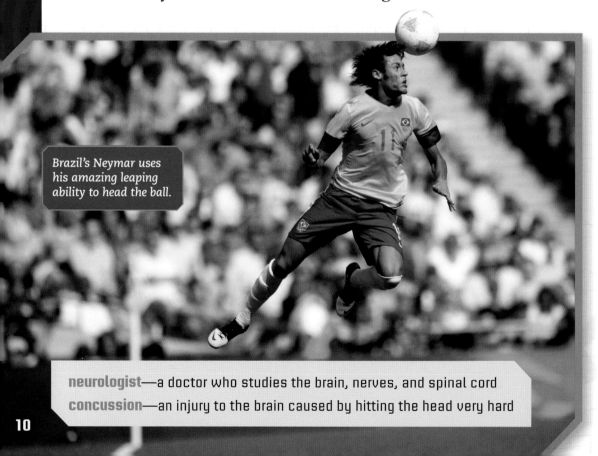

Brazil's Neymar uses his amazing leaping ability to head the ball.

neurologist—a doctor who studies the brain, nerves, and spinal cord
concussion—an injury to the brain caused by hitting the head very hard

Abby Wambach (14) has scored more goals in international competition than any player, man or woman.

Symptoms of a concussion include headaches, memory loss, and emotional problems. The more concussions a person has, the worse the long-term effects.

Young players are most at risk, according to scientists studying concussions. The U.S. Soccer Federation listened to the science. In 2015 new rules for youth leagues say players under 10 cannot head the ball.

GOAL DECISION SYSTEMS:
Eliminating Ghost Goals

Video referees on the Hawk-Eye system monitor games closely.

HAWK-EYE
INNOVATIONS

During a 2010 World Cup match against Germany, one of England's midfielders fired on goal. The shot hit the crossbar and sailed downward. Germany's goalie grabbed the ball and kept playing. England's players, thinking they had scored, started celebrating. The referee signaled nothing, though, so play continued. However, video replays showed the ball landing behind the goal line before bouncing out.

This is an example of a "ghost goal." It's a goal not counted even though it went in. Ghost goals are also those that referees mistakenly count as scores even though they don't actually cross the line.

Technology now offers help. Some top soccer leagues are adding "goal decision systems." One, called Hawk-Eye, aims six or more high-speed cameras on each goal area. They track the ball from different angles. If the whole ball crosses the goal line, the system buzzes a watch on the referee's wrist to signal a score.

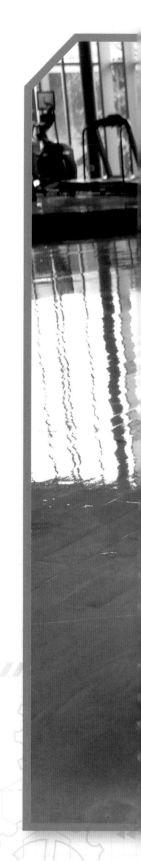

Companies are developing soccer balls with coaches built right in. These "smart balls" are regulation size and weight. They feel and fly like regular balls. Their covers, though, are lined with tiny sensors. Motion detection technology tracks their movements. The sensors measure speed, spin, distance, and force. They also count touches and dribbles.

A smart ball can send data to a computer or smart phone. Players can then use that information to experiment with their kicks. The program lets them see how they've improved over time. The ball can fuel friendly competition as players compare their soccer skills. The smart ball also indicates the time and intensity of play.

The Adidas miCoach Smart Ball represents the future of soccer equipment.

WEARABLE TECHNOLOGY: Wired for Soccer

Today top players and teams use wearable technology to perfect skills. **Monitors** are built right into practice and game gear. The gear helps athletes play smarter and harder.

Wearable tech analyzes the body's activity. An athlete's heart rate, speed, and side-to-side movement are tracked. Players' jumping ability and even how hard they hit the ground after a tackle are also recorded. Workout data allows coaches and trainers to create drills for players depending on their positions. A forward might run sprints. A defender can do drills that work on back-pedaling.

monitor—a device that shows information

Some wearable technology can pinpoint a player's position on the field. Computer software then records the players' movements in detail. After a game, a coach uses a computer to look at how the team worked together on the field. For example, the coach can see where players are bunching up too much on offense and make adjustments.

CHAPTER THREE

ENGINEERING

ROBOTICS:
Soccer in a Box

Footbonaut is a **robotic** machine shaped like a large cube. It acts like a big batting cage for soccer players. Instead of pitching softballs, though, it serves up soccer balls.

German midfielder Melanie Leupolz practices her skills in a Footbonaut training session.

The Footbonaut costs $2.4 to $3.5 million.

Footbonaut helps improve the reflexes of soccer players. A player stands in the middle of the machine's playing surface. A double-chirp and flashing red light signal what opening the pass is coming from. The player has to react and control the ball. She then shoots it into whatever opening in the walls flashes a green light.

Controls can be set to deliver the ball at different speeds and spins. Passes also pop out at different heights so the player has to handle the ball with feet, chest, or head. Footbonaut can be loaded with 200 soccer balls to keep a player hopping.

robotic—working like a machine that can do the work of a person and that is either controlled or works automatically

EVOLVING EQUIPMENT:
The History of the Soccer Ball

Soccer balls have changed over time. Long ago, balls for soccer-like games were made out of pigs' bladders. Today they are sleeker, tougher, and probably smell better.

Soccer Ball Timeline

1855
Charles Goodyear creates the first rubber soccer ball.

1862
H. J. Lindon invents a ball with an inflatable rubber bladder.

1872
The English Football Association announces soccer ball standards: **Circumference** 27–28 inches, weight: 13–15 ounces, and an "outer casing of leather or other approved materials."

1940
On wet fields, players complain traditional leather gets soggy. Designers start experimenting with **synthetic** materials. Their goal is to make the ball more waterproof.

circumference—the length of a line that goes around something

synthetic—something that is made by people rather than found in nature

aerodynamics—the ability of something to move easily and quickly through the air

The Brazuca ball was in play in a 2014 World Cup match between Belgium and Russia.

1970
The Adidas Telstar is put in play at the World Cup in Mexico. It consists of 20 white panels and 12 black panels.

1986
A ball made of all synthetic materials is used at the World Cup for the first time.

2014
The Brazuca ball is used in the World Cup in Brazil. It has only six panels. NASA (National Aeronautics and Space Administration) tests the ball in its wind tunnels. The purpose is to check the **aerodynamics**.

CHAPTER FOUR

ARTS

FASHION DESIGN:
The Art of the Uniform

Players and fans take great pride in the uniforms of their favorite teams. The colors and designs are important parts of a team's **identity**. They often share interesting background about the country or city the team represents. Companies such as Nike also pay big bucks for players to wear their **logos**.

Club America (right) has the Nike logo and eagle feathers on their uniforms.

Mexico's Club America is an artistic example of weaving identity into a jersey. The team's uniform design includes eagle feathers. These symbols are reminders of fierce Aztec warriors from Mexico's past.

The national women's team of Canada wears that country's color of deep red and a maple leaf with pride.

Shelina Zadorsky (4) of Canada and Lindsey Horan (9) of the U.S.

identity—qualities or beliefs that make people or groups unique
logo—a visual symbol of a company

Rio Ferdinand played on the English national soccer team. When not playing for the national team, he was a captain on Manchester United. Starting at age 11, Ferdinand also studied ballet. He said dancing helped him develop more balance and body control on the soccer field.

Other superstars such as Cristiano Ronaldo and Lionel Messi are also good dancers. Hope Solo, a goalkeeper for the U.S. Olympic and Women's National Team, even appeared on the TV show *Dancing with the Stars*.

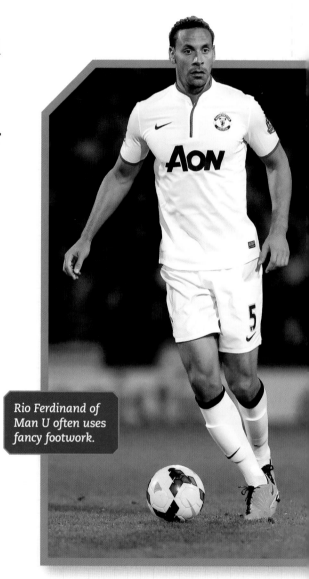

Rio Ferdinand of Man U often uses fancy footwork.

Lionel Messi of FC Barcelona routinely moves like a dancer.

Dancers can spot the similarities between moving to music and making moves with a soccer ball. Both activities require timing and technique but also balance and power.

The Soccer Jam Skills Program makes a direct dance-soccer connection. It uses musical rhythms to teach youth players footwork. By "dancing with the ball" they practice ball-handling moves. The exercise helps players build confidence in both feet.

CHAPTER FIVE

MATHEMATICS

GEOMETRY:
Math Near the Goal

A breakaway is a thrilling soccer play. It is a high-speed chess match between goalkeeper and attacker. They must make snap decisions.

Goalkeepers must calculate the angles, and that means geometry. Geometry is the mathematics of shapes and sizes. It also deals with the positions of objects in space.

When an attacker with the ball closes in, goalkeepers face a **three-dimensional** dilemma. Those dimensions are left and right, up and down, and forward and backward. If keepers simply stay on the goal line, an attacker has more open net to shoot at. Instead, keepers usually counter-attack. Facing an attacker, they come partway out of the goal. They try to take away an attacker's good angles for easy shots. A rule of thumb for good positioning is to draw a line from each goal post to the ball to form a triangle. Using that rule, keepers can position themselves to split the angle.

The power of a Megan Rapinoe kick is a weapon unto itself in any situation.

three-dimensional—having or seeming to have length, width, and depth

Penalty kicks bring up a different field of mathematics: **probability**. Probability measures how likely it may be that something will or will not happen.

Researchers study the statistics of soccer penalty kicks. This kick gives an attacker a free shot against the goalie. These blasts can reach speeds of 125 miles (201 km) per hour. With no time to react, most goalies try to outguess the kicker. Often they decide to either dive right or left to block the kick.

Argentina's Juan Riquelme blasts one toward the goal.

Spain's David Villa, at right, takes a penalty shot.

However, researchers found goalies should stop guessing. They had a greater probability of making a block if they stayed in the center of the goal. Researchers looked at thousands of penalty kicks and determined when the goalkeeper was most likely to make a save. Chances of a block jumped from 13 percent to 33 percent when the goalie stayed in the center and reacted to the shot.

People around the world think of soccer as "The Beautiful Game." It is also a great way to use science, technology, engineering, the arts, and math to explore how the world works.

probability—how likely or unlikely it is for something to happen

GLOSSARY

aerodynamics (air-oh-dy-NA-miks)—the ability of something to move easily and quickly through the air

circumference (sur-KUHM-fur-uhnss)—the length of a line that goes around something

concussion (kuhn-KUH-shuhn)—an injury to the brain caused by hitting the head very hard

drag (DRAG)—the force created when air strikes a moving object and slows it

fundamental (FUHN-duh-men-tuhl)—one of the basic, important parts of something

identity (eye-DEN-i-tee)—qualities or beliefs that make people or groups unique

logo (LOH-goh)—a visual symbol of a company

Magnus effect (MAG-nuhs uf-FEKT)—a force produced by differences in air pressure around a spinning object

monitor (MON-uh-tur)—a device that shows information

neurologist (NOO-rahl-uh-gist)—a doctor who studies the brain, nerves, and spinal cord, known as the nervous system

probability (PROB-uh-bulh-uh-tee)—how likely or unlikely it is for something to happen

robotic (ROH-bot-ik)—working like a machine that can do the work of a person and that is either controlled or works automatically

synthetic (sin-THET-ik)—something that is made by people rather than found in nature

three-dimensional (THREE–duh-MEN-shun-uhl)—having or seeming to have length, width, and depth

READ MORE

Bodden, Valerie. *Soccer.* Making the Play. Mankato, Minn.: Creative Education, 2016.

Mahoney, Emily. *The Science of Soccer.* New York: PowerKids Press, 2016.

Rogers, Amy B. *Soccer: Science on the Pitch.* Science Behind Sports. New York, Lucent Press, 2018.

INTERNET SITES

Use FactHound to find Internet sites related to this book.

Visit www.facthound.com

Just type in 9781543530407 and go.

Super-cool stuff!

Check out projects, games and lots more at
www.capstonekids.com

INDEX